Driving by the woods

woods

Echoes of life

Muktanjali Arya

CONTENTS

DEAR ONES

LOVE

PARENTHOOD

AGING

OBITUARY TO COVID

Author's Note

Hello Mum Dad, my life partner, sonnies, sisters, friends, brother, in laws, nieces, nephews...everyone out there, for whom I feel and who (may/may not) feel for me.

I sit down and compile my poems...Finally! Whoosh!

So, his is how it started.... my journey, I mean, from writing diaries to again poems. I always wrote what I was feeling but, never saved those writings for future. Sounds naïve! I know or is there Déjà vu feeling for you? Tough times and emotional moments bring out the writer in us. So, I wrote my diary daily when my kids were young and I was working professionally (dying of Mother's guilt, which hasn't left me even today). The schedule, same daily grind interspersed with joy, excitement, anger, frustration, guilt...all made it to my diary. Later, it gave way to a poetic form, wherein feelings sailed onto paper in rhythm, rhyme and stanzas. Once downloaded from my mind and heart on to a piece of paper, there was a spring in my walk. This piece of paper is a God gift or should I say human gift, for souls like me. This is Goddess Saraswati in true sense, to be touched to forehead with respect, so that its contents flow into us or vice versa.

Each and every poem conveys my heartfelt emotions and feelings for that person or persons or thought, which will resonate with the readers too. And there is no element of fiction. Everything has actually happened and I'm sure has happened in many of your lives too. So, a strong connect will be felt.

Happy reading.

Acknowledgements

With a heart full of love, hope and gratitude, I thank each and every person who has touched my life and helped me evolve in a person I am today.

All my write ups go under a surgeon's knife, coder's sharp eye, business administrator's attention to miniscule details, critical care specialist's critical expertise and radiologist's observant, hawk eyed scrutiny. Oof! But the final approval is my Dad's call, who is all of these in one, and my guiding force in heaven, my biggest critic, Mum.

So, you can see that I must acknowledge in same order, hubby Prafull Arya, sonny Dhruv, sonny Utkarsh, sis Diptimala Agarwal, sis Reemanshu Bansal and of course, dad Gopal Das Goel and mum Kailash Goel.

My list is endless but, incomplete, without acknowledging my children's grandma, Amma, Urmila Arya, in heaven, for taking care of them, sister in law, Juhi Arya, the glue that keeps the family together, my dearest brother Sanjiv Goel and my dear friends.

About the Author

Muktanjali Goel Arya, doctor by profession, is a Microbiologist and Infection control specialist with almost three decades of clinical experience. Writing came naturally to her... from writing diary to penning emotions in poetic form. Emotions is a universal language and understood by one and all. Whoever reads her poems, feels a strong connection and memories come rushing back. Besides that, reading is her passion and she enjoys travelling. And she is a yoga enthusiast, pursuing it for more than two decades, which she started when she was teaching in a medical college and her children were really small. She likes to encourage others into taking up yoga. She likes to pick new hobbies from time to time. She was born, brought up and educated from Lady Hardinge Medical College & University College of Medical Sciences in Delhi and now resides in Ludhiana, Punjab. Born to educated parents in a family with two sisters and brother, she values relationships and most of her writings are on the same. Being married into a big family, relationships became even more important for her.

ABOUT THE BOOK

Books are magic. They tempt you to step into an unknown or known world and start living other's lives vicariously. But here I am presenting a known world. Close your eyes and get that Déjà vu feeling that this has happened before.

Live those sunshine, mostly happy, rarely sad moments again. Immerse into the colors of life from childhood to adolescence, then adulthood to aging. Let's buckle up and go on this emotional drive together. Your life moments will flash past you with memories of mom, dad, sisters, brothers, friends, nieces and nephews. Experience those birthdays and anniversaries again. This ride will zip past your childhood, growing up, falling in love, birth of your first child, bringing them up, empty nest and aging. Not to be forgotten, Covid time, which brought our world to a standstill. But we humans have a great capacity and we arose from the ashes like Phoenix.

Emotions have a universal language and understood by one and all. These feelings, especially the intense ones, get an expression in our mother tongue. So, you will find hindi language words at few places.

Fasten your seat belts and let me take you along on this ride or as they say in Punjab, let's go on a gedi.

Dear Ones

I wish I had all my dear ones together under one roof so that I could see them all the time.

From Mother to Son

*That's my first born, my elder son, now grown up. All events
are true. He gave us a really hard time as a kid. But that's what
makes for lifelong glorious, cherishable memories…right?*

Friday, the 13th, it should have been!
Announced you, with your trademark mischievous grin.
But, que sera sera! whatever will be, will be,
Saturday, the 14th, it had to be.
Wailing, you arrived,
7.8 pound bundle, to our glee.
He looks bored, our little one,
needs fresh air, your Papa declared.
Barely 7 days into this world, rolling up my eyes I said,
doesn't that sound weird?
My invocations were futile, fell on deaf ears,
First brush with outside world, it was yours, it appears.
"Don't let them sleep", seemed to be your life's aim,
Happen to sleep, if they, wake up at 4, was your game.
Feeding you, playing with you, thinking about you, that's
what life was how,
Totally in love we were, besotted by you, now.
Balancing on chair on stool, you stood, prying to open the
door,

Shush! Gently I tiptoed to catch you, became my daily chore.
Potatoes you liked, to my dismay, everything else was fail,
Kept trying with unbridled passion, but to no avail.
Found a friend in your little brother,
Protective you were, like no other.
Time went by, computer and physics became your passion,
Caring, sharp, intelligent boy you are, on any topic ready to
hold discussion.
Far far away land, you have chosen to go,
But, you carry our values, our teachings, I know,
Always time for us in your busy schedule, you have dear,
Never miss a day, our calls, never, that's how much you care.
Being a parent, is an adventure, purest form of love it is,
We are lucky to have you both, with you in it, life is bliss.

———⊸∘⊷———

Perfect You Are

Kind hearted, gentle soul, that's my second born, younger son.
A mother's heart wants to protect her child from this big bad
world, but she can only support, help and love. Rest is in that
child's hands, who is a grownup adult now. But, that's mother
love!

Why don't you give something to this poor boy?
Tugging at my shirt, accusing look in eyes, said he.
Don't encourage beggary, blah! blah! my logic was no fun.
Cold hearted appeared I, to your tender soul, my son.

Breezed into our lives, our younger one, a waft of fresh air.
Your chatty chatter lit up our days and hearts dear.
A person's person are you, a charmer, my boy.
Mingling with strangers with ease, to my joy.

Wagging his tail, jumping with delight is your Bruno, a stray.
Pained were you, sent to a shelter as he was carried away.

Deviation in my voice, slightest even, so easily you perceive.
Sensitive are you, reading body language comes naturally to
you.

I love you my angel, but there is fear too.
Entering into this big bad world now, are you.
Sadness, heartbreaks! Stay away! speaks a mother's heart.
But, stay as you are sonny, perfect you are.

I'M YOUR SHADOW

Written this poem for my father, whom I call Daddyji, on Father's day with a wish that I had inherited his Gift of gab.

"Do I talk too much?" asks who,
"You do Dad" I say, because that's you.
Born with the gift of gab, you, my Dad,
Why didn't you pass this gift to me, I'm mad.
Are you a genius or a magician,
Conjuring up a joke, a story for every situation.
How do you do that Dad, I'm in awe!
Your logic, your reasoning continue to amaze me.
Your organised office, even medicine cabinets (how do you do that!) are a sight,
But nothing can match your shining shoes and hand washed white.
Born with rebellious streak, sharp intelligent handsome lad,
Yeah! That's my Dad,
Listened with rapt attention to your childhood stories with palms on face,
Sometimes I wonder how granny kept up with your pace!
You did your law, then MBA, then something then something, I heard,
Kept on studying till I was born, were you a nerd!

Not so it seems, as playing cricket was also a passion,
Making friends, travelling were also your bastion.
Tough times don't last, tough people do, they say,
That's my Dad, pray.
You and Mom's selfless love for us, unflinching faith in
supreme,
Has kept us siblings together as a strong team.
Spitting image God made me of yours,
Not only face, but palms, feet and fingers too are yours.
(even sweet tooth Dad)

Found a Friend

Ludhiana looked like a cemented city to me as we had moved from Jolly Grant, a heavenly place in Uttarakhand, with two small kids in tow. At this stage in life, making new friends seemed difficult or I should say, not possible. But life had other plans for me.

So, this is it! Said I, looking around at the city cemented,
No friends, no foes, arriving with my little kids at the house rented.
Time for new friends, I said nay,
But friends are made in heaven, they say.
Sailed into my life Kavita, kindling a new friendship,
What camaraderie! What rapport! In this new place, I found companionship.
Kids grew up, greys lurked in our hair, we were not getting any younger,
Years flew by, but our bond grew stronger and stronger.

My Guide for Life

Here's my Dad aka Daddyji and I'm his spitting image. Once my nephew joked that I am his grandpa with bindi.

Your little finger is crooked, it has a bend,
Exclaimed my dear ole friend.
My sweet slumber was broken,
You mean that! I had spoken.
And admiringly I looked at my fingers and small square hands,
That's my papa looking at me, there in my hands.
Always there in my laughter,
He is there in my eyes twinkle,
Even in my forehead wrinkle.
He is there in my mirror every day,
Though we live faraway.
So much love and blessings you always give,
In my heart is where you live.

MY ANGEL

Here comes my younger son, my angel again when he turned eighteen. Eighteen, the magic number of entering adulthood but, with rights and responsibilities. A mother only wishes that her child's wishes come true.

9.18 struck the clock
Lo! Behold! What a sight!
Our little hero had arrived, our lives' delight.
My bunny rabbit, My Angel, I said.
My handsome lad, my stylish boy, I said.
Your non-stop chatter,
Your friendly banter,
Your caring ways,
Your straight forwardness,
Your humane touch,
Your love for life.
Mesmerized and touched and enriched our lives in so many
ways.
Thats our Utkarsh,
My Kushu bro.
Always our little Hero.
May all your heart's desires come true.

That's a mother's wish with a rainbow hue,
But many midnight lamps you have to burn.
For success you want to earn,
As Eighteen you turn.

My Sister, My Delight

Childhood memories come back in waves. These waves are bitter sweet. Sometimes, a smile lits up your face, then there is a yearning to go back in time and relive those moments. Here, I am remembering my younger sister, her birth and growing up.

Tender age of four was mine,
When white as snow with glow and shine,
Chubby cheeks sailed into our hearth,
The cutest prettiest bundle of joy, ever on earth.
Tender age of two was Molly,
Awestruck amazed at this roly poly.
Juju Juju was what she muttered,
So, that is what she will be called, everyone uttered.
While growing up, she kept everyone on their toes,
She was a delight for both friends and foes.
Her elephant like memory and easy grasp,
This beauty with brains made everyone gasp.
I know her for her caring, loving and gentle ways,
My li'l sis, our Mom's Raju, is always positive, with no nays.
I wish her the best of life's hue,
May all her heart's desires come true.

Our Pride

My younger sister again! She was lucky to inherit Dad's gift of gab and continues to make us proud. All of us have that someone in the family who shines and we glow in her/his radiance.

Snow paled in comparison!
Why isn't cotton so soft?
Bundle of joy had arrived that summer,
Everyone's darling was here.
Quick witted charmer, she grew up into,
Inherited (dad's) gift of gab.
Mantle of energy is what she wears,
Sprinkling joy wherever she nears.
Like a phoenix she rises every time,
Her badges of honour multiplying.
Delve into my eyes' abyss,
Pride! Only Pride! you will find my little sis.

My First Love

My niece, my brother's daughter, who was first next generation child in the family. So, she became special and everyone's dearest. Being Bua and unmarried at that stage, I was witness to these cherished and precious moments. Lucky me!

Where are my candies, Bua?
Forgot to keep money again?
Tugging at my dress, you implored.
Large, innocent eyes fluttered, your Bua was floored.
Dainty little you, always a charmer.
First born, our Gen Next torch bearer.
Oh my delightful pretty niece!
Bawling you arrived, mesmerising one and all.
Bowl with spoon (your mom trying to feed you milk) and
dancing Dad, was definitely a sight.
Drinking milk or spraying rather, was it? Am I right!
Peering down at the little girl, bewildered was she.
Came for admission, smartly you replied with glee.
All alone you came! That's a first one for me (said the teacher).
(You were 2 & half & went inside a school near our house)
Beauty with brains you grew up into.
Giggling with you, laughing at your jokes.
Your dancing with grace, are memories I cherish.

Dadi's Gori, Bua's Tippi, Dada's delight.
My confident doc, faraway you flew (to USA).
Making us proud always, that's you.
My dear niece Arushi, remember Bua loves you.

Fun and Frolic

It is always fun and frolic time with friends. This happens to be an invite which I had sent to my lovely gang.

Hey! Next round of kitty is here again.
Fun, food & frolic time! Time to entertain.
What say! Let's bring it on with a bang.
With the best in town, our own Guys & Gals gang.
Some will meet, some will be missed.
That's the beauty of our group, everyone is reminisced.
Time, date & venue are under review,
Please tolerate my rhyme, as you always do.
Hey! Next round of kitty is here again.
Fun, food & frolic time! Time to entertain.
What say! Let's bring it on with a bang.
With the best in town, our own Guys & Gals gang.
Some will meet some will be missed.
That's the beauty of our group, everyone is reminisced.
Time, date & venue are under review,
Please tolerate my rhyme, as you always do.

FRIEND

That's FRIEND for you.

Laughter tinkles, happiness abounds,
Energy sprinkles, positivity abounds,
Spreading joy and cheer,
Who is it? hear, hear!
Ever helpful, always there,
A friend, proudly on sleeves I wear.

FRIENDS & SISTERS

This poem just describes my first impressions on meeting my 5 MBBS friends. Thereon, we became a gang of 6, friends and sisters for life.

Ashu, Amita, Deepti, Kanika, Nidhi (I say in one breath),
that's how I rattle off names of my friends dearest,
How we met, bonded for life, jogging my memory, closing my eyes quickly, what if I forget lest.
Cold coffee anyone, bellowed a girl, 2 days into college, its music to my ears,
Tall, caring, pretty, prim and proper, that's Kanika; girl you gave me a chance to escape my ragging fears.
Back to anatomy hall, to my dissection table, conjured up a cute, innocent, shining face,
Childish, cracking jokes & fighting too, Nidhi she is, I tried to keep pace.
Ding dong goes the bell, lunchtime finally & whom do I meet,
A pretty face, naughty smile & music in her voice, high on emotions, is Ashu, at her seat.
There are two more there, to my glee,
Sparkling eyes, innocent at heart, intelligence at its best & tubelight too, Deepti is what I see.

Tall, model like, beautiful types, smiling at me,
Loving & caring, this girl, who loves to repeat her advices to
her loved ones, Amita, is she.
So, there we were, six in a troupe,
Through thick and thin we sailed all these years, stood the
test of time as one group.

STAY AS YOU ARE

The charmer, my younger one, comes back again and turns twenty-one. A mother hopes that this world is not able to change his love for life and optimism.

Utkarsh, always my Kushu, as 21 you turn,
Feelings of tender ache and happiness galore, surface and churn.
My sonny, my friend and my bro too,
Like a gentle caressing breeze, into my life you flew.
Full of life, your optimism sprinkles,
Non-stop chatter, your sweet laughter tinkles.
Kindness and sharing, are your forte my son,
Learnt these from you, must thank you a ton.
Retain your charm, your exuberance, your innocence, as years in life pass through,
Because all this and much more, make you YOU.

STRANGERS TO FRIENDS FOR LIFE

As there is seven-year itch in marriage, I believe that if a friendship lasts more than seven years, then friends become like relatives.

On a lighter note, this is what I have to say. "The ride is on. And remember that the ride was not smooth and there are still hiccups. But we keep going. And beware, we are entering a new phase. As in any family, we have mausi, bua, phupha, didi, bhaiyya, infact all relationships are developing."

No more strangers, friends no more,
Oh! What did I say? But, came from my heart's core.
Joys and sorrows too, we share now,
I often wonder all this happened how.
Fear of being judged has gone, it's no more,
I'm telling you soon this story is going to be folklore.
From strangers to acquaintances, from friends to family, we have come a long way,
It's my hope and wish that this is for forever stay.
So, guys and gals! What do you say!

HOLDING US TOGETHER

All of us have friends, some a handful, some many. But there are some friends who hold friends' group together. They are like glue.

Friendship makes you wealthy,
more than money can buy.
Friendship brings health,
more than meditation can try.
Lucky am I, found a friend like you.
Benevolent and caring, always ready to help, that's you.
Social, amiable with organising skills,
Vocabulary falls short for a pleasant pure soul like you.
You are the force that binds our group, oh boy!
Wishing you good health, peace and joy.

LOVE

The only thing that we never get or give enough is love.

MY LIFE MATE

Written on our 26th marriage anniversary, in this poem I go back to meeting my life mate for the first time to the birth of our kids. I adore his caring ways and at the same time tease him for some of his habits.

Dear, we have come a long way,
In this life's June, July and May.
Strolling in the gardens at India Gate,
And you became my lifelong mate.
Then came Dhruv, filling our life with newfound joy,
He turned out a quiet, intelligent, naughty boy.
Lo! Behold came talkative, caring, handsome Utkarsh,
And our joy knew no bounds.
26 years have just flown past,
But we both held high, our mast.
Joys and sorrows sailed in equal measure,
These happy sad memories became our treasure.
I love not only your loving caring ways,
I admire not only your eternal optimistic ways,
But also, your not listening to what I'm saying ways.

I adore not only your ever smiling, sweet, charming
merriment,
But also, your stubborn temperament.
Many many more years will come and be gone,
Our love and trust will always stay strong.

Ode to My Love

This is my ode to love, the life story of my life mate.

What should I write? Racking my brain,
But ideas desert me, everything in vain.
Most special person, someone you love, is called? One word
for that!
Scratching my head, I put on my thinking hat.
2nd Jan, 1994! Does that ring a bell dear?
It does! It does! I hear.
That beautiful day, we first met, you sailed into my life.
Happened to be your birthday too & I became your wife.
Attentively listened to stories of your birth, your childhood
saga,
Amma would tell repeatedly, as a mother does, their child's
raga.
A shy child, beautiful and brilliant,
In life's situations, you turned out resilient.
Your interest in reading, love for Physics & Math,
Becoming a doctor, a surgeon, you found your path.
We found more love, more joy, as Dhruv Utkarsh lit up our lives,
Two junior versions, both nature wise look wise.
Your patience, optimism, cracking mini jokes all the time
(which irritate me sometimes),

Pareshan mat ho! Ho jayega! Is your favourite line.
Simple, gentle, soft spoken, unaware of worldly game,
Caring, sharing, selfless, loving is thy name.

⸻ ⬥ ⸻

Stood the Test of Time

25years! Quarter of a century, that's silver, a precious metal but, less than gold and platinum...right! So, preciousness increases with years, or does it? I ponder. Written for a committed couple, my sister and her life partner.

25 years! How time flies, says everyone,
Does it really fly, I ponder.
How two educated girl and boy, tie the knot,
Without knowing each other, I wonder.
But then, marriages are made in heaven, say our wise,
There must be some truth in it, let me not criticise.
So, how's the flight I persist?
Turbulences, weather changes happen,
Rough are they but, then comes the smooth part too,
Let your other half grow, let him/her shine in their own hue.
Soon, you'll be joined by more of your own (your kids) in this bliss,
Journey will be more turbulent but, most beautiful then.
A doctor girl from Delhi, a gentle, kind, loving soul,
passionate, mental strength of a bull,
Met a doctor boy from Agra, intelligent compassionate soul,
humane too, with attractive pull.

Fell in love, got married and 25 years flew past with the blink of an eye,
Joined by two strapping handsome boys on the way,
toppings on the pie.
Celebrate love, celebrate togetherness, celebrate sharing,
you both,
Because life is love, love is life, that's the ultimate oath.

———⋙∘⋘———

My Feelings on Paper

28 years of our marital life! And down the memory lane I go. I had crossed the number of years spent in my parental home finally. Oft repeated joke between us.

What will I do without you,
My life mate! my partner!
Quite often I ponder,
As these days my thoughts wander.
28 years have flown past! Really!
Does seem like an era, clearly.
Now, I have crossed years spent in childhood hearth,
As so often I told you in mirth.
Only then shall I belong to you. hear! hear!
Nothing but a playful banter dear.
In joy and in sorrow,
In sunshine and in darkness,
From twinkles to wrinkles,
From youth to greys,
Stood by me through all.
Fulfilling all saat phera vows, I do recall.
Taken when we were so so young,
Two people in love, life had just begun.
Down the memory lane I go, if you must insist.

Hard times far and few, I see,
But only love, joy and sweetness persist.
Let's hold onto each other,
As we move on in this life and beyond, together.

———◦◦———

MARITAL ODYSSEY

Another one on this lifelong unknown adventure ride called marriage. It's breathtaking and astounding, if with someone you love.

Love at first sight!
Sounds fairy tale like! right?
Hmm! But did it happen?
Nope! Comes the swift reply,
Missed the bus? Poor thing! Now, don't deny.
Wake up, stop day dreaming dear,
Fairy tales are made right here.
Bus is waiting, board and hop along,
Hand in hand, in odyssey lifelong.
Is the journey smooth, I ask,
Odysseys are never smooth, you silly, I get a rebuke.
There are speed breakers, near misses, weather changes,
But if you are lucky then it's by a fluke.
Look at the big picture dear,
On a lifelong, unknown adventure with someone by your side,
With someone you love, you share, you care,

It becomes an awesome ride.
Never loosen your grip, keep holding hands tight,
And as the time goes past, everything seems right.

Matches Are Made in Heaven

Sometimes we have to actually believe that matches are made in heaven. Bollywood comes live before our eyes.

Made for each other, matches are made in heaven
blah, blah…is it true, they say,
Looking at them both, we said, yay!
Cool, awesome are you, inspiring is your optimism,
Always making friends, viewing world with a happy,
colourful prism.
Ready to pitch in for friends, at any time,
You brought us, our group together into a harmonious
musical chime.
Mast, jhakaas..describes you in Bollywood lingo,
We are lucky we found you…Bingo!
Made for each other, that's you two.

PARENTHOOD

Unescapable truth

Once a Mom, always a Mom

Once a Papa, always a Papa

Once a Parent, always a Parent.

OUR FIRST LOVE

First born is every couple's first love and every girl remembers her mother on becoming mother herself. So, with my mom's words, I remember by elder son's birth, his mischief and his virtues.

Now, he is grown up, independent and mature enough to take his own decisions. That makes us proud. But, in our heart, he is still that little naughty boy for whom good weather was "Mummy aaj mausam mausam hai", keys were "chaibee", soft was "gayak", who cried when his mom left for work (I missed you even more), whose Papa brought his passion (computer) home, who danced when his little brother was born, who always ran outside to play in sandpit (made by his Papa) every time the door opened and so on (the list is endless). He is all this and much more.

My mom said "Doosra janam hota hai, Maa banane par Daisy",
What is she saying, I thought! Gosh! Has she gone crazy.
But, as always, she was right,
When before me was my blue-eyed boy, what a sight.
You kept us busy day and night,
Though we tried with all our might,
So active, you refused to sleep at night.

As if that wasn't enough, you shook and woke me with an
innocent smile,
Uff! Its only 4 a.m., you charming beguile.
Alas! Lying spread eagle on the floor is the driver,
Thrown out mercilessly from the toy car you broke, poor
rider.
Now, what is this! Standing on a stool balancing on a chair,
Trying to open the door, boy, you are giving me a nightmare.
Trying to leave home for job became a job itself,
Crying your heart out you clung to me & I cried myself.
Breaking toys led to constructing them, did I mention,
Then your Papa got a toy (computer) which became your
lifelong passion.
Patience is your virtue, I noted, when you waited for your
little brother's arrival,
Not a drop of jealousy as he was no rival.
You were protective, he looked upto you,
Now, Dhruv Utkarsh were a strong team of two.
Just loving and playing with your little brother,
You waited for those little trips (to neighbourhood shop) on
Sundays with your mother.
Returning from hospital one day,
What do I see, to my dismay.
Perched atop a tree are you, my little monkey,
My heart skipped a beat, seeing my naughty spunky.
All doors were closed by Amma (your dadi), as she ventured
out,
Turning around (you gave her the scare of a lifetime) she saw
you standing, from a window you had wriggled out.
Eating only potatoes, you fussy eater, was bad,

Huffing and puffing running around the lawn feeding you
was mad,
You almost gave hypertension to your mom and dad,
But, thank God, you turned out a handsome bright lad.
Not just to me, but for everyone who knows you,
You are gentle and caring,
You are sharp and intelligent,
You are loving and logical (at the same time),
And we are so proud of you,
You are a great son, a tremendous blessing,
And a wonderful gift to the world.

———⊂○⊃———

Making of a Mom

Arrival of bundle of joy leading to endless years of unselfish love, makes a Mom.

So many years have flown by! Really!
Yes! Years and years have gone by. Clearly!
Faraway was I, in that bottomless pit.
My very own pensieve, with memories it lit.
Bawling you arrived, with all your might.
Caught unawares was I, it was love at first sight.
Overnight I changed, transformation was real.
Selfless loving woman arose, feeling was surreal.
Lightening had struck, happy go lucky ambitious girl took a backseat.
In awe was I, feeling little bundle's hands and feet.
Embarked on this journey, to the road ahead oblivious.
Had all spices, no less than masala movie nonetheless.
Unaware they existed, such emotions unearthed.
Extremes of love, joy, anxiety and what not came with your birth.
Flooded was I, in emotional tsunami.
Thanks dear, for making me your Mommy.

IMPERFECTLY PERFECT – A MOTHER'S JOURNEY

Every mother's dilemma! It's not easy being a mother.

Have I been a good mother?
A thought does peekaboo, so often.
A working mother's dilemma!
Or every mother's, I guess.
Have I given them time?
Have I instilled right values?
Have I raised them well?
These "have I s", grow relentlessly.
Overflow and flood me ceaselessly.
A Good Mother! Will they remember me as?
Independent, confident, caring are you.
That's what you molded us into.
Saw love and respect abound between you two (mom & dad).
These life's lessons watching, we grew.
Mom, you are the best! they sang in chorus.
Music to my ears, golden words priceless.
Nothing but, a mother's guilt, I realised.

Pre-defined gendered notions of nurture, idealised.
Humans we are, no mother is perfect.
With my doubts put to rest (for the meantime), peacefully I
slept.

MY SONNIES ARE HOME

There is a constant battle between wanting our kids to stay little and the love of watching them grow. Then, comes a day they leave home. We empty nesters yearn for those bygone years and wait eagerly for their next trip home.

Your house is a mess, she insisted,
But I'm loving it, I resisted.
Empty bags, shoes, chargers everywhere, where's the order,
This is my haven, with a bemused look, I ignored her.
Familiar chatter, squabbles, laughter reign,
My home is alive again.
Mess to you, is bliss for me.
Chaos that appears, is calm for me.
Birds that had flown,
are now back home.
Soar back again, they will soon,
But rejoice in the sunshine, for its a boon.
Attachment with detachment, often hear about,
Trying hard to learn, there's no doubt.
Let me soak in the moment, please allow,
My sonnies are back home again now.

LET THEM GROW

What do you want to become when you grow up, doctor or engineer? Such a strong déjà vu feeling you had. Right! Your interests are unimportant as there are just two moulds to fit into. So decide.

Medical or Non medical!! Beta, what's your plan?
Oft heard cliche it is, please put a ban.
Going by this favourite phrase, do only doctors and
engineers exist?
Hearing for the zillionth time, are there only two professions,
I resist.
Give them soil, give them water, please let in some air too,
Let these saplings grow in open air, don't strangle with your
view.
Open their mind's window, your love and support is the key,
And soon they'll prosper, make you proud and grow into
healthy humane tree.

ITS MAGIC

Grandparenthood is the time to rejoice with more time and less responsibilities. So, soak in the moment.

Time to rejoice
Time to soak in the moment
Its magic she says
As she peers closely in those round innocent eyes, a
reflection of her
At loss of words is he
First time in life
So overwhelmed
So joyous
Such surge of emotions
This lil angel has brought he wonders
She wails, she pouts, she frowns
She chuckles, she giggles, she smiles
Holding her lil finger, stroking her cheek, caressing her hair
Dawns the realisation
Grandpa I am now
Grandma I am now

AGING

Bones creak, knees pain, memory betrays us, but aging has its own charm. Live it, feel it.

Fifty is a Number

Age is just a number. But my Maths is poor.

Fifty is just a number, they say
Ten times five is fifty
Add one to forty nine and lo! you turn fifty
But is fifty just a number, I ask
Fifty winters, came and went
Numbing bones, engulfing darkness, empty roads
Fire warmed our hearth and hearts
Ray of sunshine here and there
Fifty springs followed soon
Blooming flowers, melody in air, singing hearts
Make way for heat, sun at its menacing best
Bide your time dear
Caress of gentle breeze
Drizzle of cool sprinkle is near
What about the sleepless nights
Fear of failing, broken hearts
Consigned to oblivion Eh!
Tranquil nights and peaceful days
Merry making jovial days in equal measure
Fifty years gone by Really!!
Golden moments remain

Sieved my memories actually!
Fifty years of evolving
Fifty wrinkles razzle dazzle
I spread love and laughter
But love myself first
So, is fifty really a number, I wonder.

GREYS AND WRINKLES

Those younger to you oft remind you of your age and I'm sure that we did the same.

"You resemble my aunt" said she,
Jolted out of reverie, was me.
Hmm! That's how to her, I must look,
With my greys in temples and forehead wrinkles,
I laugh and my crow's feet crinkles.
Age is chronology, my calendar, the history I bear,
Age is just a number, so oft I hear.
Hey! Number it is but, numbers countless,
Childlike behaviour with childhood friends, is doubtless.
College friends mean college jokes,
Number increases amongst professional folks.
Giant or lilliput, but child is there inside,
Tries to leap out, but we manage to hide.
Entire life to societal norm, we conform,
Ah! Sixty, you are old, they discern,
But, twenty is young, you must learn.
Young at heart, not in body, so what!
Let the little one jump out, why let it rot.
So, age is just a number, it's what you feel,
Makes you wiser, no doubt, but never let it steal your zeal.

OBITUARY TO COVID

I thought that only an obituary for covid is befitting.

BACK TO NEST

Covid times become live again. Families coming together under one roof, lockdowns leading to pure air and all types of animals coming out where they had hidden from human fear. What was unimaginable became a reality.

Trudging their bags, coming back to their hearth,
Goodness gracious! What calamity has befallen on our mother earth.
Masked faces, anxious eyes, dread in the air,
This is 2020, The Year of Fear.
Avoid strangers, has been the teaching, But, shun your own, became the new preaching.
But, as they say, something good comes out of something bad,
Those who had flown away from their nests, the birds were back in their pad.
Birds sang, nature swayed, as change is the only constant,
We looked in disbelief, but lived in the moment.
Children were home, families once again together, simply wow,
What was unimaginable was a reality now.